Bead Knitted Amulet & Coin Purse Patterns

This book is intended to provide clear instruction in the creation of the bead knitted amulet and coin purses featured in this book. Every effort has been made to ensure that the contents of the instructions are accurate. Due to individual knitting styles/skills and differing tools/materials, finished products may vary slightly.

The book is intended to inspire craft ideas, but if readers are not proficient in a skill necessary for a given pattern, we advise that they refer to an instructional book designed to teach a specific technique.

Editor: Renee Gomez-Smith
Pattern Proofreader: Cindy Husley
Photography: Michelle Corrine

Library of Congress Cataloging-in-Publication Data

Gomez-Smith, Renee
Bead Knitted Amulet and Coin Purses/Renee Gomez-Smith
"Love to Bead book"
ISBN

Published by Love to Bead Press
300 SW 6th St., Grants Pass, Or USA 97527
© 2009 by Renee Gomez-Smith

Table Of Contents

Dedication:
To my three beautiful daughters who have given me so much love and
my husband for his loving support in putting together this book.

In memory of Cesar Gomez and my dearest father, Ronald Abram

A Brief Introduction

The amulet purses presented in this book reflect the era of the 1920s, but are created to be worn as necklaces. The word "amulet" is derived from the Arab word "hamala," which means "to carry." An amulet can be anything that is carried on the body at any given time.

Many people choose to wear these knit amulet purses with small charms or something of sentimental value inside them. A friend mentioned that she carries small amounts of her favorite perfume on cotton balls in her knit amulet purses. Another friend mentioned that she carries a small amethyst stone in her knit amulet to bring her inner peace and enlightenment.

In the early twentieth century, the beaded bags imported to the U.S. from Europe had elaborate patterns and were difficult and time consuming for the amateur bead worker to duplicate. By the 1920s, beaded apparel and purses were the height of fashion. Instruction books of the time show numerous patterns for "swag" purses (<u>Beads on Bags: 1800s - 2000</u>, Shiffer Publishing, 2000).

"In our own time the fashioning of beaded articles is not a fad; it is more than a love of adornment - it is artistry; there is a certain charm about the combining of colors which are made more beautiful by the play of light on the surface of the beads. We wish to leave you with this thought; that beadwork is always worthwhile; though fashion may change there is always a return to the beaded; the artistic work of your hands today will give you much satisfaction while the vogue is strong, and a work of art always lives, becoming enhanced by age in both value and sentiment." -Emma Post Barbour, <u>1924 New Bead Book.</u> Chicago: National Trading Company.

Beaded Knit Purse Patterns: Helpful Tips

Materials: The patterns featured use size 11/0 seed beads from the Czech Republic or size 3 Bugle beads, size 8 pearl cotton thread and size 0000 knitting needles. It is helpful to use seed beads that are strung in hanks. A small crochet hook, a darning needle and a flexible eye needle will also be handy. Experiment using different sized beads and other threads. Size FF silk thread, or size 20 Cebelia thread also work well (Cebelia will cause beaded fringe to twist slightly). The finished sizes of these purses will vary slightly depending upon the gauge of your knitting, size of the beads and type of threads used.

Getting started: Transfer the beads onto pearl cotton cord. If your beads are strung, pull one side of the beads out of the hank's knot, and tie an overhand knot with the seed bead thread around the pearl cotton. Slide the beads carefully over the knot onto the pearl cotton. Remove any mis-shaped or poor-quality beads as you go. If your beads are unstrung, use a bead spinner or, using a fine flexible eye needle, thread the beads onto pearl cotton (and be patient!). Cover one end of the double-pointed knitting needles with something to protect yourself from getting poked. Suggestions: Attach metal or rubber earring backs or small corks to your needles, or glue large accent beads onto your needles. Read all instructions prior to knitting. Always make sure to get all of the thread and beads needed to complete a pattern at the same time to avoid dye lot problems. Most purse patterns have beads on both sides of the purse (inside and outside) and are knitted in one piece with one or two seams. Flaps are usually knitted first, then the purse pattern follows.

Thread Management: To prevent thread from tangling, place the pearl cotton thread spool in a small sandwich bag, only slide the beads down the cord about 3 feet at a time. It is best not to transfer more than one hank of seed beads onto the pearl cotton because it becomes unmanageable to keep sliding beads down. Keep the beads close together on the cotton cord. Place all of your cord (including the spool in its small baggy) into a larger plastic bag to keep cord/beads clean. If your thread with beads tangles hopelessly, or a knot is discovered in the spool of cord, try to untangle the knot(s). If that does not work, transfer the seed beads onto a thin thread (sewing thread will work) from the section of pearl cotton in question. Then, tie the other end of the thin thread onto a new portion of the spool of pearl cotton thread. Transfer all of the beads and proceed. Note that in all of the patterns, the bead is slid into place between knit stitches. If you drop a stitch, don't panic. Get into an area with good lighting. Hold the dropped stitch with a spare knitting needle until you locate your crochet hook (use a tiny one). Pick up the stitch, being careful not to twist stitches.

Finishing Techniques: Whip stitch purse sides with right sides together using a darning needle. Turn the purse inside out. To make your strap: Use a length of about 30 inches of the beads left on the cotton cord, or desired length. For a stronger strap consider using a soft, flexible beading wire. Thread ends through larger accent beads using the flexible eye needle (space accent beads with seed beads) and attach to purse sides. Dab knots with fray-resistant glue. Attach charms or decorative beads to purse front or side, as desired.

Attaching purses to purse frames: Whip stitch purse sides with right sides together using your darning needle.   Do not sew sides completely to the top or the purse frame will not open. Sew side seams until they measure 1/3" below where frame will begin. Attach purse body to purse frame by completing the following: Thread double through a size 10 beading needle.   With purse body right side out, sew from inside center of knitted purse top to back of inside center of purse frame top. Continue to sew through holes on purse frame (backstitching) to the far side of the purse frame. Cut another 3 foot section of beading thread, thread double through needle, and continue by sewing from center again toward the other side of purse frame. Repeat on other side of frame. Secure all thread ends with knots and glue. Line purse if desired. Cover the inside edges of the purse frame by gluing on brocade ribbon, if desired. Attach the purse strap (chain or beadwork).

Care of beaded purses: Hand wash in cool water with a gentle detergent. Re-shape or block as needed. Dry flat. It is recommended that purses be protected from bright sunlight when not in use. Ask about the colorfastness of beads when you purchase them. Color-lined beads may lose their inside color.

7

11

13

14

❧ *Patterns* ☙

Simply Lovely

Note that this purse is knitted in one piece with two side seams. You begin working on the back side of the purse and end on the front side. Beads will be both on the outside and inside of the purse.

Supplies:

> 1 hank of size 11 seed beads
> 1 spool of pearl cotton thread
> 1 pr. size 0000 knitting needles
> 8-20 decorative beads

Instructions:

1. Transfer beads onto pearl cotton thread. Place rubber stoppers on the ends of knitting needles.
2. Cast on 18 stitches.
3. Rows 1 - 2: k across
4. Rows 3 - 4: k2, sl1,* k1, sl1*, repeat *, end with k2. (Optional, or k across). This gives the purse the top edge of beads.
5. Rows 5 - 10: k3, sl1 bead, repeat and finish with k3.
6. Rows 11 - 16: k3, sl2 beads, repeat and finish with k3.
7. Rows 17 - 22: k3, sl3 beads, repeat 4 x and finish with k3.
8. Rows 23 - 28: k3, sl4 beads, repeat 4 x and finish with k3.
9. Rows 29 - 34: k3, sl5 beads, repeat 4 x and finish with k3.
10. Rows 35 - 40: k3, sl6beads, repeat 4 x and finish with k3.
11. Rows 41 - 46: k3, sl7 beads, repeat 4 x and finish with k3.
12. Rows 47 - 52: k3, sl8 beads, repeat 4 x and finish with k3. You're halfway finished!
    (Note: now you begin working on the front side of the purse).
13. Rows 53 - 58: repeat rows 47 - 52.

14. Rows 59 - 64:   repeat rows 41 - 46.
15. Rows 65 - 70:   repeat rows 35 - 40.
16. Rows 71 - 76:   repeat rows 29 - 34.
17. Rows 77 - 82:   repeat rows 23 - 28.
18. Rows 83 - 88:   repeat rows 17 - 22.
19. Rows 89 - 94:   repeat rows 11 - 16.
20. Rows 95 - 100:   repeat rows 5 - 10.
21. Rows 101 - 102:   repeat rows 3 - 4.
22. Rows 103 - 104:   repeat rows 1 - 2, as desired.
23. Bind off. See Finishing Techniques, p.3.

Lacey

Please note that odd rows with larger loops are the front (outside) of the purse. Even rows will be the inside of the purse.

Supplies:

> 1 hank of size 11 seed beads
> 1 spool of pearl cotton thread
> 1 pr. size 0000 knitting needles
> 8-20 decorative beads

Instructions

1. Transfer beads onto pearl cotton thread. Place rubber stoppers on the ends of knitting needles. Cast on 18 stitches by knitting on.
2. Rows 1 - 4: k across.
3. Rows 5 - 10: k3, sl1 bead, repeat 4 x and finish with k3.
4. Rows 11 - 16: k3, sl2 beads, repeat 4 x and finish with k3.
5. Rows 17 - 22: k3, sl3 beads, repeat 4 x and finish with k3.
6. Rows 23 - 28: k3, sl4 beads, repeat 4 x and finish with k3.
7. Rows 29 - 34: k3, sl5 beads, repeat 4 x and finish with k3.
8. Rows 35 - 40: k3, sl6 beads, repeat 4 x and finish with k3.
9. Rows 41 - 46: k3, sl7 beads, repeat 4 x and finish with k3.
10. Rows 47 - 52: k3, sl8 beads, repeat 4 x and finish with k3. You're halfway finished!
    Now you begin working on the front side of the purse. The large loops are only on the front side.
11. Row 53: k3, sl30 beads, repeat, k3 sl35 beads, k3 sl30 beads, repeat.
    Row 54: k3, sl8 beads, repeat 4 x and finish with k3.
    Row 55: k3, sl30, repeat 4 x and finish with k3.
    Rows 56 and 58: even rows repeat row 54.
    Row 57: repeat row 55.
12. Rows 59,61 and 63: k3, sl25 beads, repeat 4 x and finish with k3.

Rows 60, 62 and 64: repeat rows 41 - 46.

13. Rows 65, 67 and 69: k3, sl20 beads, repeat 4 x and finish with k3.
    Rows 66, 68 and 70: repeat rows 35 - 40.

14. Rows 71, 73 and 75: k3, sl15 beads, repeat 4 x and finish with k3.
    Rows 72, 74 and 76: repeat rows 29 - 34.

15. Rows 77, 79 and 81: k3, sl10 beads, repeat 4 x and finish with k3.
    Rows 78, 80 and 82: repeat rows 23 - 28.

16. Rows 83, 85 and 87: k3, sl3 beads, k3 sl3, k3 sl8 beads, k3 sl3 beads, k3 sl3, finish with k3.

17. Rows 84, 86 and 88: repeat rows 17 - 22.

18. Rows 89 - 94: repeat rows 11 - 16.

19. Rows 95 - 100: repeat rows 5 - 10.

20. Rows 101 - 104: repeat rows 1 - 4.

21. Bind off. See Finishing Techniques, p.3.

Dottie Loop

Note that the large loops will only be on one side of the purse (the front, outside only). See Pattern sequences. It is helpful to mark your stopping point if you are putting your work down for awhile. Check your work after each row to be sure that you achieve the polka dot pattern correctly with beads on the front side of the purse. Try this purse without the large loops on the front side by repeating in reverse order rows 1 - 38.

Supplies:

        1 hank of size 11 seed beads
        1 spool of pearl cotton thread
        1 pr. size 0000 knitting needles
        8-20 decorative beads

Instructions

Pattern sequence

When this symbol appears [*], repeat this pattern: * k1, sl1, k 2, sl1, k1 * (XOXXOX). When this symbol appears [•], repeat this pattern: • k2, sl1, k2 • (XXOXX)

1. Transfer seed beads onto the pearl cotton thread. Place rubber stoppers on the ends of knitting needles.
2. Cast on 18 stitches.
3. Rows 1 - 4: knit across.
4. Row 5 - 6: k 5, sl1, k4, sl1, k4, sl1, k 5.
5. Row 7 - 12: k 5, sl2, k4 , sl2, k4, sl2, k 5.
6. Row 13: k1, repeat *, sl3, repeat *, sl3, repeat *, sl3, repeat *, end with k1.
7. Row 14: k 5, sl3, k4, sl3, k4, sl3, k 5.
8. Row 15: k1, repeat •, sl3, repeat •, sl3, repeat •, sl3, repeat •, end with k1.
9. Row 16: repeat row 14.
10. Row 17: repeat row 13.
11. Row 18: repeat row 14.
12. Row 19: k1, repeat •, sl4, repeat •, sl4, repeat •, sl4, repeat •, end with k1.
13. Row 20: k 5, sl4, k4, sl4, k4, sl4, k 5.

14. Row 21: k1, repeat *, sl4, repeat *, sl4, repeat *, sl4, repeat *, end with k1.
15. Row 22: repeat row 20.
16. Row 23: repeat row 19.
17. Row 24: repeat row 20.
18. Row 25: k1, repeat *, sl5, repeat *, sl5, repeat *, sl5, repeat *, end with k1.
19. Row 26: k 5, sl5, k4, sl5, k4, sl5, k 5.
20. Row 27: k1, repeat •, sl5, repeat •, sl5, repeat •, sl5, repeat •, end with k1.
21. Row 28: repeat row 26.
22. Row 29: repeat row 25.
23. Row 30: repeat row 26.
24. Row 31: k1, repeat •, sl6, repeat •, sl6, repeat •, sl6, repeat •, end with k1.
25. Row 32: k 5, sl6, k4, sl6, k4, sl6, k 5.
26. Row 33: k1, repeat *, sl6, repeat *, sl6, repeat *, sl6, repeat *, end with k1
27. Row 34: repeat row 32.
28. Row 35: repeat row 31.
29. Row 36: repeat row 32.
30. Row 37: k1, repeat *, sl7, repeat *, sl7, repeat *, sl7, repeat *, end with k1.
31. Row 38: k 5, sl7, k4, sl7, k4, sl7, k 5.
32. Row 39: k1, repeat •, sl7, repeat •, sl7, repeat •, sl7, repeat •, end with k1.
33. Row 40: repeat row 38.
34. Row 41: repeat row 37.
35. Row 42: repeat row 38 (You're halfway finished!).
36. Row 43: k1, repeat •, sl25, repeat •, sl35, repeat •, sl25, repeat •, end with k1.
37. Row 44: k 5, sl7, k4, sl7, k4, sl7, k 5.
38. Row 45: k1, repeat *, sl25, repeat *, sl35, repeat *, sl25, repeat *, end with k1.
39. Row 46: repeat row 44.
40. Row 47: repeat row 43.
41. Row 48: repeat row 44.
42. Row 49: k1, repeat *, sl20, repeat *, sl25, repeat *, sl20, repeat *, end with k1.

43. Row 50: k 5, sl6, k4, sl6, k4, sl6, k 5.
44. Row 51: k1, repeat •, sl20, repeat •, sl25, repeat •, sl20 repeat •, end with k1.
45. Row 52: repeat row 50.
46. Row 53: repeat row 49.
47. Row 54: repeat row 50.
48. Row 55: k1, repeat •, sl15, repeat •, sl20 repeat •, sl15, repeat •, end with k1.
49. Row 56: k 5, sl5, k4, sl5, k4, sl5, k 5.
50. Row 57: k1, repeat *, sl15, repeat *, sl20, repeat *, sl15, repeat *, end with k1.
51. Row 58: repeat row 56.
52. Row 59: repeat row 55.
53. Row 60: repeat row 56.
54. Row 61: k1, repeat *, sl10, repeat *, sl15, repeat *, sl10, repeat *, end with k1.
55. Row 62: k 5, sl4, k4, sl4, k4, sl4, k 5.
56. Row 63: k1, repeat •, sl10, repeat •, sl15, repeat •, sl10, repeat •, end with k1.
57. Row 64: repeat row 62.
58. Row 65: repeat row 61.
59. Row 66: repeat row 62.
60. Row 67: k1, repeat •, sl3, repeat •, sl3, repeat •, sl3, repeat •, end with k1.
61. Row 68: k 5, sl3, k4, sl3, k4, sl3, k 5.
62. Row 69: k1, repeat *, sl3, repeat *, sl3, repeat *, sl3, repeat *, end with k1.
63. Row 70: repeat row 68.
64. Row 71: repeat row 67.
65. Row 72: repeat row 68.
66. Rows 73 - 78:   k 5, sl2, k4, sl2, k4, sl2, k 5 (6 rows).
67. Rows 79 - 80:   k 5, sl1, k4, sl1, k4, sl1, k 5 (2 rows).
68. Rows 81 - 85:   k across
69. Row 86: Bind off. See Finishing Techniques, p.3.

Sachet

Note that on this pattern, you will be knitting the purse in one piece beginning at the bottom and working toward the top. There will be one seam located at the back of the purse. Large loops will only be on the outside front of your beaded purse. To make a pattern strand. Use a 2 yard section of thread. With a flexible eye needle, thread 15 seed beads, one decorative bead, 15 seed beads. Repeat 10 times. Set aside pattern strand.

Supplies:

> 1 hank of size 11 seed beads
> 1 spool of pearl cotton thread
> 1 pr. size 0000 knitting needles
> 8-20 decorative beads

Instructions

1. Transfer beads to cotton cord. Place rubber stoppers on the ends of knitting needles.
2. Cast on 36 stitches.
3. Rows 1 - 4: k across.
4. Rows 5 - 6: k1, sl1, repeat across ending with k1.
5. Rows 7 - 8: k across
6. Row 9: k3, cast off one (by slipping second stitch over third and off the right needle), repeat across. (Rows 9 and 10 will create buttonholes). (24 stitches).
7. Row 10: k2, in second stitch increase one, repeat across, end with k1 (36 stitches).
8. Rows 11 - 12: k across.
9. Rows 13 - 14: repeat row 5.
10. Rows 15 - 26: k3, sl1, repeat across ending with k3.
11. Rows 27 - 32: k3, sl3, repeat across ending with k3.
12. Row 33: k3, sl25, repeat across ending with k3.
13. Row 34 - 36: k3, sl4, repeat across ending with k3.
14. Row 37: k3, sl30, repeat across ending with k3.

15. Row 38 - 40: k3, sl4, repeat across ending with k3.
16. Row 41: k3, sl30, repeat across ending with k3.
17. Rows 42 - 44: k3, sl6, repeat across ending with k3.
18. Row 45: k3, sl30, repeat across ending with k3.
19. Row 46 - 48: k3, sl6, repeat across ending with k3.
20. Row 49: k3, sl35, repeat across ending with k3.
21. Rows 50 - 52: k3, sl6, repeat across ending with k3.
22. Row 53: k3, sl35 , repeat across ending with k3.
23. Rows 54 - 56: k3, sl5, repeat across ending with k3.
24. Row 57: Cut knitting strand off. Knit using pattern strand: k3, sl15 seeds + 1 teardrop + 15 seeds, repeat across ending with k3. All of pattern strand will be used. Tie off pattern strand. Continue using knitting strand.
25. Rows 58 - 59: k3, sl5, repeat across ending with k3.
26. Rows 60 - 61: k3, sl3, repeat across ending with k3.
27. Rows 62 - 63: k3, sl2, repeat across ending with k3.
28. Rows 64 - 69: k3, sl1, repeat across ending with k3.
29. Row 70: k across.
30. Row 71: k3, bind off one, repeat across. (Rows 71 and 72 will create buttonholes).
31. Row 72: k2, in second stitch increase one, repeat across.
32. Row 73 & 74: k across.
33. Rows 75 & 76: k1, sl one bead, repeat across ending with k1.
34. Rows 77 & 78: k1, sl one bead, repeat across ending with k1.
35. Row 79 -81: k across.
36. Row 82: bind off.
37. With wrong sides together, neatly whip stitch the back seam of purse together using a darning needle and pearl cotton thread. Using a darning needle, thread fine ribbon through buttonholes at top and bottom of purse so that the ends meet in the front of the purse. Add large hole beads to ends of ribbon and tie overhand knots at the end of ribbon. Trim ribbon and dab with fray resistant glue. See Finishing Techniques, p.3.

The Dress

Note that this purse is knitted in one piece with two side seams. You begin working on the back of the purse and end on the front side.

Supplies:
>   1 hank of size 11 seed beads
>   1 spool of pearl cotton thread
>   1 pr. size 0000 knitting needles
>   8-20 decorative beads

Instructions
1. Transfer beads onto cotton thread. Place rubber earring stoppers on the ends of knitting needles.
2. Cast on 18 stitches.
3. Rows 1 - 2: k across.
4. Row 3:   K1, sl1 , * k2, sl1*, repeat * across, end with k1.
5. Row 4: k across.
6. Row 5:   k2, sl1 , * k2, sl1*, repeat * across, end with k2.
7. Row 6: k across.
8. Row 7: k3, sl1 , * k2, sl1*, repeat * across, end with k3.
9. Row 8: k across.
10. Row 9:   k4, sl1 , * k2, sl1*, repeat * across, end with k4.
11. Row 10: k across.
12. Row 11: k 5, sl1 , * k2, sl1*, repeat * across, end with k 5.
13. Row 12: k across.
14. Row 13: k 6, sl1 , * k2, sl1*, repeat * across, end with k 6.
15. Row 14: k across.
16. Row 15: k 7, sl1 , * k2, sl1*, repeat * across, end with k 7.
17. Row 16: k across.

18. Row 17: k 8, sl1 ,* k 2, sl1*, repeat, end with k 8.
19. Row 18: k across.
20. Row 19: k 9, sl1 , end with k 9.
21. Rows 20 - 23: k across. Note: You've just completed the back top area of the doll's dress.
22. Rows 24 - 25: k 9, sl1 , end with k 9.
23. Rows 26 - 27: k 6, sl1 , k3, sl1 , k3, sl1 , end with k 6.
24. Rows 28 - 29: k3, sl1 , *k3, sl2* , repeat * 2x, k3, sl1, end with k3.
25. Rows 30 - 31: k3, sl2 , *k3, sl3* , repeat * 2x, sl2, end with k3.
26. Rows 32 - 33: k3, sl3 , *k3, sl4* ,repeat * 2x, k3, sl3, end with k3.
27. Rows 34 - 35: k3, sl4 , *k3, sl4* , repeat * 3x, end with k3.
28. Rows 36 - 41: *K3, sl5 *, repeat * across, end with k3.
29. Rows 42 - 47: *k3, sl6 *, repeat * across, end with k3.
30. Rows 48 - 55: *k3, sl7 *, repeat * across, end with k3.
31. Rows 56 - 65: *k3, sl8 *, repeat * across, end with k3.
32. Repeat rows 65 - 1 in descending order.
33. Bind off. Using your darning needle, whip stitch purse sides with right sides together. Turn the purse inside out (it may be necessary to leave the top half of one side open, then whip it together after it is turned inside out). See Finishing Techniques, p.3.

Copyright 2000 all rights reserved.   Pattern revised 2009.

Lantern

Note that on this pattern, you will be knitting the purse in one piece beginning at the bottom and working toward the top. There is only one seam located at the back of the purse. To make a pattern strand: take a two-yard section of pearl cotton thread. Using a flexible eye needle, thread 15 seed beads, one decorative bead, then 15 seed beads. Repeat 10 times. Set aside pattern strand.

Supplies:

> 1 hank of size 11 seed beads
> 1 spool of pearl cotton thread
> 1 pr. size 0000 knitting needles
> 8-20 decorative beads
> 8 3x6mm Spear or tear-shaped beads

Instructions

1. Transfer beads onto cotton thread. Place rubber stoppers on the ends of knitting needles.
2. Cast on 9 stitches.
3. Row 1: k across.
4. Rows 2 - 3: k1, sl1 , repeat across (7 times), ending with k1.
2. Row 4: k1 - in this stitch increase 1, sl1 , repeat across (7 times), ending with k1, inc 1. (Remember, you sl the bead after you inc as you begin to k the next stitch. There will be 2 stitches between each bead).
6. Row 5: k2, sl1 , repeat across, end with k2.
7. Row 6: k2 - in 2nd stitch inc 1, sl1 , repeat across, end with k2, inc 1.
8. Row 7: k3, sl1 , repeat across, end with k3.
9. Row 8: k2 - in 2nd stitch inc 1, k1, sl1 , repeat across (7 times), end with k2 - in 2nd stitch inc 1, k1.
10. 10. Rows 9 - 10: k4, sl1, repeat across, end with k4.
11. Rows 11 - 12: k4, sl2, repeat across, end with k4.
12. Rows 13 - 14: k4, sl3, repeat across, end with k4.
13. Rows 15 - 16: k4, sl4, repeat across, end with k4.
14. Rows 17 - 18: k4, sl5, repeat across, end with k4.
15. Rows 19 - 22: k4, sl6, repeat across, end with k4.
16. Rows 23 - 28: k4, sl7, repeat across, end with k4.

17. Rows 29 - 34:   k4, sl8, repeat across, end with k4.
18. Rows 35 - 40:   k4, sl7, repeat across, end with k4.
19. Rows 41 - 46:   k4, sl6, repeat across, end with k4.
20. Rows 47 - 52:   k4, sl5, repeat across, end with k4.
21. Rows 53 - 54:   k4, sl4, repeat across, end with k4.
22. Rows 55 - 56:   k4, sl3, repeat across, end with k4.
23. Row 57:   k1, dec 1, k1, sl3, repeat across, end with k1, dec 1, k1.
24. Row 58:   k3, sl3, repeat across, end with k3.
25. Rows 59-62:   k3, sl2, repeat across, end with k3.
26. Row 63:   k1, dec 1, sl2, repeat across (7 times) ending with k1, dec 1.
27. Row 64:   k2, sl2, repeat across, end with k2.
28. Row 65:   dec 1, sl2, repeat across, end with dec 1.
29. Row 66:   k1, sl1, repeat across, end with k1.
30. Row 67:   using the pattern strand, k1, slide a sequence including 15 seed beads, 1 spear bead and 15 seed beads, k1, repeat across (7 times), end with k1.
31. Row 68:   k1, sl1, repeat across, end with k1.
31. Row 69:   k across.
32. Row 70:   bind off.
33. Thread a 12-inch length of thread into a darning needle. With wrong sides together, neatly whip stitch the back seam of purse together to the center portion of the purse (do not stitch the entire seam together!). Leave string. Thread another 12-inch section of thread into darning needle. Loop thread into each of the first stitches on the bottom of the purse, leaving a 5-inch tail. Pull ends of thread to tighten purse bottom. Knot thread ends together neatly. Turn purse inside out (right side should now be out). Thread back seam thread into darning needle again. Tighten thread and whip stitch the remaining length to the top of the purse together. Knot thread in place. To make your strap: See Finishing Techniques, p.3. **Pattern variation:** Due to the fact that the purse opening is so tiny, it is nearly impossible to place objects in it. If you wish to create a more useful purse, do not decrease in rows 57 and 63. This will change the shape of the purse slightly and create a wider opening on the purse top.

27

Diamonds

Supplies:

> 1 hank of size 11 seed beads
> 1 spool of pearl cotton thread
> 1 pr. size 0000 knitting needles
> 8-20 decorative beads

Instructions

1. Transfer seed beads onto cotton cord. Place rubber stoppers on the ends of your knitting needles.
2. Cast on 15 stitches.
3. Rows 1 - 8: k across.
4. Rows 9 - 10: k3, sl1, repeat across, end with k3.
5. Rows 11 - 12: k3, sl2, repeat across, end with k3.
6. Rows 13 - 14: k3, sl3, repeat across, end with k3.
7. Rows 15: k3, sl4, * k2, in second stitch inc 1 stitch, k1 , sl4 * repeat sequence within * 2 x, end with k3.
8. Row 16: k3, sl4, *k2 inc in 2nd st, k2 sl4* repeat * 3x, end with k3.
9. Row 17: k3, sl5,* k2 in second stitch inc 1 stitch, sl1, k3 *, repeat sequence within * 2 x , end with k3.
10. Row 18: * k3, sl5, k3, sl1*, repeat * 2 x , k3, sl5, end with k3.
11. Rows 19 - 20: * k3, sl4, k3, sl2 *, repeat * 2 x , k3, sl4, end with k3.
12. Rows 21 - 22: * k3, sl3, k3, sl3 *, repeat * 2 x, k3, sl3, end with k3.
13. Rows 23 - 24: * k3, sl2, k3, sl4 *, repeat * 2 x, k3, sl2, end with k3.
14. Rows 25 - 26: * k3, sl1, k3, sl5 *, repeat * 2 x, k3, sl1, end with k3.
15. Rows 27 - 28: * K3, sl2, k3, sl4 *, repeat * 2 x, k3, sl2, end with k3.
16. Rows 29 - 30: * k3, sl3, k3, sl3 *, repeat * 2 x, k3, sl3, end with k3.
17. Rows 31 - 32: * k3, sl4, k3, sl2 *, repeat * 2 x, k3, sl4, end with k3.
18. Rows 33 - 34: * k3, sl5, k3, sl1 *, repeat * 2 x, k3, sl5, end with k3.
19. Rows 35 - 36: * k3, sl4, k3, sl2 *, repeat * 2 x, k3, sl4, end with k3.
20. Rows 37 - 38: * k3, sl3, k3, sl3 *, repeat * 2 x, k3, sl3, end with k3.

21. Rows 39 - 40: * K3, sl2, k3, sl4 *, repeat * 2 x, k3, sl2, end with k3.
22. Rows 41 - 42: * k3, sl1, k3, sl5 *, repeat * 2 x, k3, sl1, end with k3.
23. Rows 43 - 44: * K3, sl2, k3, sl4 *, repeat * 2 x, k3, sl2, end with k3.
24. Rows 45 - 46: * k3, sl3, k3, sl3 *, repeat * 2 x, k3, sl3, end with k3.
25. Rows 47 - 48: * k3, sl4, k3, sl2 *, repeat * 2 x, k3, sl4, end with k3.
26. Rows 49 - 50: * k3, sl5, k3, sl1 *, repeat * 2 x, k3, sl5, end with k3.
    (You have now completed the back of the purse!)
27. Rows 51 - 52: Repeat rows 49 - 50.
28. Rows 53 - 83: Repeat rows 48 - 18 in that order.
29. Row 86: k3, sl4, * k2 stitches together, k4, sl4 *, repeat * 2 x, end with k3.
30. Row 87: k3, sl4, * k2 stitches together, k3, sl4 *, repeat * 2 x, end with k3.
    Row 88: k3, sl3, * k2 stitches together, k2, sl3 *, repeat sequence in * 2 x , end with k3.
31. Row 89: k3, sl3, * k2 stitches together, k1, sl3 *, repeat * 2 x , end with k3.
32. Row 90: k3, sl3, repeat across, end with k3.
33. Rows 91 - 94: repeat rows 12 - 9 in that order.
34. Rows 95 -101: k across.
35. Bind off. See Finishing Techniques, p.3.

Zig Zag

Supplies:

> 1 hank of size 11 seed beads
> 1 spool of pearl cotton thread
> 1 pr. size 0000 knitting needles
> 8-20 decorative beads

Instructions

1. Cast on 18 stitches by knitting on, not the overhand method.
2. Rows 1 - 4:   k across.
3. Rows 5 - 6:   k3, sl1, repeat 4 x's, end with k3.
4. Rows 7 - 8:   k3, sl2, repeat 4 x's, end with k3.
5. Rows 9 -10:   k3, sl3, repeat 4 x's, end with k3.
6. Rows 11 - 12:   k3, sl4, repeat 4 x's, end with k3.
7. Rows 13 - 14: * k3, sl3, k3, sl5* repeat *, k3, sl3, end with k3.
8. Rows 15 - 16:   * k3, sl2, k3, sl6* repeat *, k3, sl2, end with k3.
9. Rows 17 - 18: * k3, sl1, k3, sl7* repeat *, k3, sl1, end with k3.
10. Rows 19 - 20: * k3, sl2, k3, sl6* repeat *, k3, sl2, end with k3.
11. Rows 21 - 22: * k3, sl3, k3, sl5* repeat *, k3, sl3, end with k3.
12. Rows 23 - 24: * k3, sl4, k3, sl4* repeat *, k3, sl4, end with k3.
13. Rows 25 - 26: * k3, sl5, k3, sl5* repeat *, k3, sl5, end with k3.
14. Rows 27 - 28: * k3, sl4, k3, sl6* repeat *, k3, sl4, end with k3.
15. Rows 29 - 30: * k3, sl3, k3, sl7* repeat *, k3, sl3, end with k3.
16. Rows 31 - 32: * k3, sl2, k3, sl8* repeat *, k3, sl2, end with k3.
17. Rows 33 - 34: * k3, sl1, k3, sl 9* repeat *, k3, sl1, end with k3.
18. Rows 35 - 36: * k3, sl2, k3, sl8* repeat *, k3, sl2, end with k3.
19. Rows 37 - 38: * k3, sl3, k3, sl7* repeat *, k3, sl3, end with k3.

20. Rows 39 - 40:   * k3, sl4, k3, sl6* repeat *, k3, sl4, end with k3.
21. Rows 41 - 42:   * k3, sl5, k3, sl5* repeat *, k3, sl5, end with k3.
22. Rows 43 - 44:   * k3, sl6, k3, sl6* repeat *, k3, sl6, end with k3.
23. Rows 45 - 46:   * k3, sl5, k3, sl7* repeat *, k3, sl5, end with k3.
24. Rows 47 - 48:   * k3, sl4, k3, sl8* repeat *, k3, sl4, end with k3.
25. Rows 49 - 50:   * k3, sl3, k3, sl 9* repeat *, k3, sl3, end with k3.
26. Rows 51 - 52:   * k3, sl2, k3, sl10* repeat *, k3, sl2, end with k3.
27. Rows 53 - 54:   * k3, sl1, k3, sl11* repeat *, k3, sl1, end with k3.
28. Repeat rows 54 - 1 in descending order (start with 54 and work backwards).
29. Bind off.   See Finishing Techniques, p.3.

Pinstripes

This purse uses 2 hanks of size 11 seed beads and 1 full ball of pearl cotton thread. An optional 1-inch deep x 2 1/2-inch wide purse frame can be used.

Supplies:

> 2 hanks of size 11 seed beads
> 1 spool of pearl cotton thread
> 1 pr. size 0000 knitting needles
> 8-20 decorative beads

Only transfer one hank of seed beads at a time (transfer the second hank later, when you are nearly out of seed beads on the yarn). You will use most of the two hanks of seed beads and an entire spool of pearl cotton thread. Note: if you will be using a frame for this purse, do not knit a flap.

Optional fringe at the bottom of the purse: Before beginning to knit, create a separate pattern strand to be set aside and used later in this pattern. Using the flexible eye needle, *string 11 seed beads, one 4 mm decorative bead (db), 10 more seed beads *. Repeat * 4 times. There will be 5 decorative beads spaced by 21 seed beads. String 61 seed beads; these will be used for row 70. String * 15 seed beads, one 4mm db, 14 seed beads * repeat * 4 times. There will be 5 4mm decorative beads spaced by 29 seed beads. String 61 seed beads; this will be used as row 74.   String * 17 seed beads, one 6mm db, 16 seed beads *. Repeat * 4 times. This will be used as row 72. String * 21 seed beads, one 6mm db, one teardrop, one 6mm db, 20 seed beads *. Repeat * 4 times. There will be 5 db sets spaced by 41 seed beads. Do not add the 61 seed beads here. This will be the beginning of your strand. Set pattern strand aside.

Optional purse flap

Save 1/4 strand of seed beads for the flap pattern strand (do not thread them onto the pearl cotton when transferring the other beads).   After threading all other seed beads onto pearl cotton cord, create the flap pattern strand by stringing the following beads using the flexible eye needle: 6 seed beads, one 6 mm decorative bead, one teardrop, one 6mm db, 16 seed beads, one 6mm db, one teardrop bead, one 6mm db, 16 seed beads, one 6mm db, one teardrop, one 6mm db, and end with 6 seed beads. There will be 3 db sets spaced by 16 beads. These are the first beads to be used when knitting the purse.

Instructions

1. Cast on 18 stitches.
2. Rows 1 - 4: k across.
3. Row 5: k6 sl6 seed beads, 1st db set, 6 seed beads, k3, sl10 seed beads, 2nd db set, 10 seed beads, k3 sl6 seed beads, last db set, then 6 seed beads, ending with k 6.
4. Row 6: k across. (This is the back side of the inside of the flap).
5. Rows 7 - 8: k3, sl1, repeat across end with k3.
6. Rows 9 - 12: k3 sl1, k3 sl2, k3 sl2, k3 sl2, k3 sl1, end with k3.
7. Rows 13 - 16: k3 sl1, k3 sl3, k3, sl3, k3, sl3, k3, sl1, end with k3.
8. Row 17: k2, inc 1 in 2nd st , sl1, *k3 sl4*, repeat * 2x, k3 s1, end with k3.
9. Row 18: k2, inc 1 in 2nd st , sl1, *k3 sl4*, repeat * 2x, k3 sl1, end with k4.
10. Row 19: k4, sl1, k1 inc 1 , k1 sl4, k3, sl4, k3 sl4, k3 sl1, k4 sl1, end with k4.
11. Row 20: k4 sl1, k1 inc 1 , k1 sl4, k3 sl4, k4 sl1, end with k4.
12. Rows 21 - 22: k4 sl1, k4 sl5, k1 inc 1 , k1 sl5 , k3 sl5, k4 sl1, end with k4. (Row 22 do not increase, end with k4 sl5, k4 sl1 and k4).
13. Rows 23 - 24: k4 sl1, *k4 sl5*,repeat * 2x, k4 sl1, end with k4.
14. Rows 25 - 26: k4 sl1, *k4 sl4*, repeat * 2x, k4 sl1, end with k4.
15. Rows 27 - 28: k4 sl1, *k4 sl3*, repeat * 2x, k4 sl1, end with k4.
16. Rows 29 - 32: k4 sl1, *k4 sl2*, repeat * 2x, k4 sl1, end with k4.
17. Rows 33 - 34: *k4 sl1*, repeat * across, end with k4.
18. Continue to instructions for purse body, skipping the cast on step.

Purse Body:

1. Cast on 24 stitches (if you will be using a purse frame).
2. Rows 1 - 8: k across (if desired, add a few more rows of plain knit here to fold over).
3. Rows 9 - 14: *k4 sl1*, repeat * across ending with k4.

4. Rows 15 - 16: * k2 sl1, k2 sl2*, repeat * across, end with k2 sl1, k2.
5. Rows 17 - 20: *k2 sl1, k2 sl3*, repeat * across, end with k2 sl1, k2.
6. Rows 21 - 26: *k2 sl1, k2 sl4*, repeat * across, end with k2 sl1, k2.
7. Rows 27 - 32: *k2 sl1, k2 sl5*, repeat * across, end with k2 sl1, k2.
8. Rows 33 - 44: *k2 sl1, k2 sl6*, repeat * across, end with k2 sl1, k2.
9. Rows 45 - 50: *k2 sl1, k2 sl7*, repeat * across, end with k2 sl1, k2.
10. Rows 51 - 56: *k2 sl1, k2 sl8*, repeat * across, end with k2 sl1, k2.
11. Rows 57 - 62: *k2 sl1, k2 sl9*, repeat * across, end with k2 sl1, k2.
12. Rows 63 - 68: *k2 sl1, k2 sl10*, repeat * across, end with k2 sl1, k2.
13. **If you are _not_ adding fringe use the following instructions:**
    Row 69 - 76: *k2 sl1, k2 sl11* repeat * across end with k2 sl1, k2.
    Proceed to rows 77 - 144.
    If you are adding fringe to the purse use the following instructions:
    Row 69: cut knitting thread from work, leaving a 6-inch tail, and set aside. Attach fringe strand so that the first db set is the 6mm, teardrop, 6mm db sequence. Continue as follows: *k2 sl1, k2 sl20 seed beads, db set, sl20 seed beads* repeat * across end with k2, sl1, k2.
    Row 70: * k2 sl20 seed beads, db set, sl20 seed beads* repeat * across, end with k2 sl1, k2.
    Row 71: *k2 sl1, k2 sl16 seed beads, db set, sl14 seed beads* repeat * across, end with k2 sl1, k2.
    Row 72: repeat row 70.
    Row 73: *k2 sl1,k2 sl14 seed beads,db set, sl14 seed beads* repeat * across, end with k2 sl1,k2.
    Row 74: Repeat row 70.
    Row 75: *k2 sl1, k2 sl10 seed beas, db set, sl10 seed beads* repeat * across, end with k2 sl1, k2.
    Row 76: Transfer the second hank of seed beads onto the pearl contton. Re-attach the knitting thread to your work. Repeat row 70.
14. Rows 77 - 144: repeat rows 68 - 1 in that order.
15. Bind off. Knot all pattern strand ends. Dab knots with glue. See Finishing Techniques, p.3.

Two-tone Diamonds

Note that this purse is knitted in one piece with two side seams. You begin working on the back side of the purse and end on the front side. Also note that in this purse, two colors of beads and pearl cotton are used to create the pattern. When changing thread color you will be knitting the first row of the new color on the inside/plain knit section. This creates a clean line/break of color across the front of the purse.

Supplies:

> ½ hank each of 2 colors size 11 seed beads
> ½ spool of 2 colors of pearl cotton thread
> 6-12 decorative beads
> 1 pr size 0000 knitting needles

Instructions

1. To transfer beads (color one) onto pearl cotton thread (color one). Repeat with the hank of color #2 seed beads and color #2 of the pearl cotton thread. Place rubber stoppers on the ends of knitting needles. Keep each spool of thread in a small baggy and all seed beads closely against each other to prevent tangling. Please also note that you should cut thread at sides when starting the next color, leaving a 8 inch tail each time. When knitting a new thread color in, it is important to knit a few stitches, then tie off threads on the side from the last color to the new color using a square knot. This will help to keep the knitting from unraveling or becoming loose. The tails will later be used to sew up the side seams.
2. Cast on 30 stitches with color #1.
3. Rows 1 - 16: k across.
4. Row 17 : * k3, sl1*, repeat * 8 times, end with k3.
5. Row 18: k across.
6. Row 19: k1 sl1,* k3, sl1 * repeat * 9 times, end with k2.
7. Row 20: k across.
8. Row 21: k2 sl1, * k3, sl1 * repeat * 9 times, end with k1.
9. Row 22: k across.
10. Rows 23 - 27: repeat rows 21 - 17 in that order. Cut strand off needles, leaving an 8-inch tail, and set #1 color

aside. Attach color #2.

11. Rows 28 - 34: using color #2, repeat rows 16 - 22.
12. Rows 35 - 41 using color #2, repeat rows 21 - 17 in that order. Cut strand off needles leaving an 8-inch tail.
    Set color #2 aside. Attach color #1.
13. Row 42. Using color #1, knit across.
14. Rows 43 - 44: (color #1) K3 sl1, repeat across, end with k3. You will have beads on both the inside and
    outside of the purse.
15. Rows 45 - 46: (color #1) k3, sl2, repeat across, end with k3.
16. Rows 47 - 48: (color #1) k3, sl4, repeat across, end with k3.
17. Rows 49 - 50: (color #1) k3, sl2, repeat across, end with k3.
18. Rows 51 - 52: (color #1) k3, sl1, repeat across, end with k3. Row 53: (color #1) knit across. Cut strand off
    needles, leaving an 8 inch tail. Set color #1 aside.
    Attach color #2.
19. Rows 54 - 65: (color #2) repeat rows 42-53. Cut strand off needles, leaving an 8-inch tail. Set color #2
    aside. Attach color # 1.
20. Rows 66 - 77: (color #1) repeat rows 42 - 53.
21. Rows 78 - 81: (color #1) knit across. (You will be finishing the bottom of the purse with these plain knit rows).
22. Rows 82 - 158: repeat rows 77 - 1 in that order repeating thread color changes.
23. Bind off. See Finishing Techniques, p.3.

Copyright 2002. Revised 2006, all rights reserved.

The Vase

Supplies:

>1 hank of size 11 seed beads
>1 spool of pearl cotton thread
>1 pr. size 0000 knitting needles
>8-20 decorative beads

Instructions

1. Cast on 18 stitches.
2. Rows 1 - 8: k across.
3. Row 9: k2 sl1, across, ending with k2.
4. Rows 10 - 12: k across.
5. Row 13: k1 sl1, *k2 sl1, repeat * across, ending with k1.
6. Rows 14 - 16: k across.
7. Row 17: k2 sl1, repeat across, ending with k2.
8. Row 18 - 20: k across (18 stitches).
9. Rows 21 - 22: k2 sl1, repeat across, end with k2.
10. Rows 23 - 24: k2 sl2, repeat across, end with k2.
11. Rows 25 - 30: k2 sl3, repeat across, end with k2.
12. Rows 31 - 36: k2 sl4, repeat across, end with k2.
13. Rows 37 - 62: k2 sl5, repeat across, end with k2. (To make a smaller purse, do 6 rows of sl5.)
14. Rows 63 - 64: k2 sl4, k2 sl4, *k2 sl5*, repeat *3x, k2 sl4, k2 sl4, end with k2.
15. Row 65: k1 inc1, k1 sl3, k2 sl4, *k2 sl5*, rep * 3 x, k2 sl4, k2 sl3, k1 inc1, k1.
(You should now have 20 stitches.)
16. Row 66: k1 inc1, k2 sl3, k1 inc1, k1 sl4, *k2 sl5*, rep * 3x, k2 sl4, k1 inc1, k1 sl3, k1 inc1, k2. (You should have 24 stitches.)
17. Row 67: k4 sl2, k1 inc1, k2 sl3, k1 inc1, k1 sl4, k2 sl5, k2 sl5, k2 sl4, k1 inc1,sl3 k1 inc1 k2 sl2,k4. (28 stitches.)

37

18. Row 68:   k4 sl2, k4 sl3, k1 inc1, k2 sl4, k1 inc1, k1 sl5, k2 sl5, k1 inc1, k1 sl4, k1 inc1, k2 sl3, k4 sl2, k4. (32 stitches).
19. Row 69:   k4 sl1, k4 sl2, k4 sl3, k1 inc1, k2 sl4, k1 inc1, k1 sl4, k1 inc1, k2 sl3, k4 sl2, k4 sl1, k4. (35 stitches).
20. Row 70:   k4 sl1, k4 sl2, k4 sl3, k4 sl4, k1 inc1, k2, sl4, k4 sl3, k4 sl2, k4 sl1, k4. (36 stitches).
21. Rows 71 - 72:   k8 sl1, k4 sl2, k4 sl3, k4 sl3, k4 sl2, k4 sl1, k8.
22. Rows 73 - 74:   k12, sl1, k4, sl2, k4 sl2, k4 sl1, k12.
23. Rows 75 - 76:   k16 sl1, k4 sl1, k16.
24. Rows 77 - 78:   knit across (36 stitches).
25. Row 79:   k32, with the yarn in the back of your work, slip the next stitch purl-wise. Move the yarn between your needles to the front of your work. Slip the same stitch back onto the left needle. Turn your work to start the next row, bringing the yarn to the purl side between the needles. You have now wrapped the stitch. Continue to next row.
26. Row 80:   k28, wrap stitch and turn (using direction from row 79.)
27. Row 81:   k24, wrap stitch and turn.
28. Row 82:   k20, wrap stitch and turn.
29. Row 83:   k16, wrap stitch and turn.
30. Row 84:   k12, wrap stitch and turn.
31. Row 85:   k8, wrap stitch and turn.
32. Row 86:   k4, wrap stitch and turn.
33. Rows 87 - 172:   You're halfway finished! Repeat rows 86 - 1 in that order. When the pattern indicates an increase stitch, decrease by knitting two stitches together instead. Pay close attention to decreases. Be sure that the staggered bead pattern rows 17 - 9 are on the front side of the purse.
34. Bind off. See Finishing Techniques, p.3.

Hearts

Note that this purse is knitted in one piece lengthwise with two side seams.

Supplies:

      ½ hank of size 11 seed beads
      1 spool of pearl cotton thread
      1 pr. size 0000 knitting needles
      8-20 decorative beads

Instructions

1.   Cast on 48 stitches.
2.   Row 1: k across.
3.   Row 2: k1 sl1, *k2 sl1*, repeat * across, end with k1.
4.   Row 3: k across.
5.   Row 4: k2 sl1, repeat across, end with k2.
6.   Row 5: k across.
7.   Row 6: repeat row 2.
8.   Row 7: k across.
9.   Row 8: repeat row 4.
10. Row 9 - 11: k2 p2 across.
11. Row 12: k2 p2, *k1 sl1, k1 p2*, repeat * across, end with k2.
12. Row 13: k2 p2 across.
13. Row 14 - 15: k across.
14. Row 16: k7 sl1, k1 sl1, k1 sl1, k across.
15. Row 17: k across.
16. Row 18: k6 sl1, *k1 sl1*, repeat * 3x, k7 sl1, k across.
17. Row 19: k across.
18. Row 20: k5 sl1, *k1 sl1*, repeat * 5x, k7 sl1, knit across.
19. Row 21: k across.

20. Row 22: k6 sl1, *k1 sl1*, repeat * 5x, k5 sl1, k2 sl1, k across.
21. Row 23: k across.
22. Row 24: k7 sl1, *k1 sl1*, repeat * 5x, k5 sl1, k2 sl2, k across.
23. Row 25: k across.
24. Row 26: K7 sl1, *k1 sl1* repeat * 6x, k5sl1, k2 sl2, k across.
25. Rows 27 - 50: You're halfway finished! Repeat rows 25 - 1 in that order.
27. Bind off. With right sides together, whip stitch one side seam. Shell stitch at top of purse: You will be spacing 4 shells (dc clusters) across back, then 4 more across the front. Attach pearl cotton at right side. 1 sc, skip 1/4 inches (approx.), 6 dc in top edge, skip 1/4 inch 1 sc, continue across. If you end exactly at the side seam - great! If not, do a few stitches to end at the side seam. Repeat across top of front side of purse ending at left side with a sc. Tie off. See Finishing Techniques, p.3.

Mini Pinstripe

Note that this purse is knitted in one piece with two side seams. You begin knitting the flap of the purse (if desired), then continue to the back of the purse, ending in the front.

Supplies:

 1 hank of size 11 seed beads
 1 spool of pearl cotton thread
 1 pr. size 0000 knitting needles
 8-20 decorative beads

Flap Instructions (optional):
Dotted Flap Instructions

1. Cast on 4 stitches.
2. Rows 1 - 2: k across.
3. Row 3: k2, sl1, k2 (4 stitches)
4. Row 4: k across.
5. Row 5: *k1 inc1 sl1*, rep * 2x, k1 inc1. (8 stitches)
6. Row 6: k across.
7. Row 7: *k1 inc1 sl1* rep * 1x, k2 sl1, k2 sl1, k1 inc1, sl1 k1 inc1. (12 stitches)
8. Row 8: k across.
9. Row 9: *k1 inc1 sl1* rep 1x, *k2, sl1* repeat * 3 x, k1 inc1 sl1,k1 inc. (16 stitches)
10. Row 10: k across.
11. Row 11: k1 inc1, sl1, *k2, sl1* repeat * 6x, k1 inc1. (18 stitches)
12. Row 12: k across.
13. Row 13: k2 sl1, repeat across.
14. Row 14: k across.
15. Row 15: k2 sl1, repeat across.
16. Row 16: k across.

17. Row 17:   k2, sl1, repeat across.
18. Proceed to Step 2 of Purse Instructions.

Purse Instructions:
1.   If not making a flap, cast on 18 stitches.
2.   Rows 1 - 8:   k across.
3.   Rows 9 - 14:   k1 sl1, *k2 sl1*, repeat * 7x, end with k1.
4.   Rows 15 - 18:   k1 sl1, *k2 sl2, k2 sl1*, repeat * 3x, end with k1.
5.   Rows 19 - 22:   k1 sl1, *k2 sl3, k2 sl1*, repeat * 3x, end with k1.
6.   Rows 23 - 26:   k1 sl1, *k2 sl4, k2 sl1*, repeat * 3x, end with k1.
7.   Rows 27 - 30:   k1 sl1, *k2 sl5, k2 sl1*, repeat * 3x, end with k1.
8.   Rows 31 - 38:   k1 sl1, *k2 sl6, k2 sl1*, repeat * 3x, end with k1.
9.   Rows 39 - 42:   k1 sl1, *k2 sl7, k2 sl1*, repeat * 3x, end with k1.
10. Rows 43 - 48:   k1 sl1, *k2 sl8, k2 sl1*, repeat * 3x, end with k1.
11. Rows 49 - 52:   k1 sl1, *k2 sl9, k2 sl1*, repeat * 3x , end with k1.
12. Rows 53 - 104:   You're halfway finished! Repeat rows 52 - 1 in that order.
13. Bind off. See Finishing Techniques, p.3.

Dotted Coin Purse

Pattern Sequence

When this symbol appears [*], repeat this pattern: * k1, sl1, k 2, sl1, k1 * (XOXXOX)

When this symbol appears [•], repeat this pattern: • k2, sl1, k2 • (XXOXX)

Supplies:

> 2 hanks size 11 seed beads
> 1 spool of pearl cotton thread
> one-2 inch wide purse frame
> chain for handle
> 1 pr size 0000 knitting needles

Instructions

1. Cast on 20 stitches.
2. Rows 1 - 8:   knit across.
3. Rows 9 -14:   k1 inc1, knit across. (You should have 26 stitches beginning on row 15.)
4. Rows 15 - 16:   k13 sl1, k13.
5. Rows 17 - 18:   k9 sl1, k4 sl2, k4 sl1, k9.
6. Rows 19 - 20:   k5 sl1, k4 sl2, k4 sl3, k4 sl2, k4 sl1, k5.
7. Row 21:   k1, repeat •, sl2, repeat •, sl3, repeat •, sl4, repeat • sl3, repeat •, sl2, repeat •, end with k1.
8. Row 22:   k 5 sl2, k4 sl3, k4 sl4, k4 sl3, k4 sl2, k 5.
9. Row 23:   k1, repeat *, sl3, repeat *, sl4, repeat *, sl4, repeat *, sl4, repeat *, sl3, repeat *, end with k1.
10. Row 24:   k 5 sl4, k4 sl4, k4 sl4, k4 sl4, k4 sl4, k 5.
11. Row 25:   k1, repeat •, sl4, repeat •, sl4, repeat •, sl4, repeat •, sl4, repeat •, sl4, repeat •, end with k1.
12. Row 26:   repeat row 24.
13. Row 27:   k1, repeat *, sl4, repeat *, sl4, repeat *, sl4, repeat *, sl4, repeat *, sl4, repeat *, end with k1.
14. Row 28:   repeat row 24
15. Row 29:   k1, repeat •, sl5, repeat •, sl5, repeat •, sl5, repeat •, sl5, repeat •, sl5, repeat •, end with k1.
16. Row 30:   k 5, sl5, k4, sl5, k4, sl5, k4, sl5, k4 sl5, k 5.

17. Row 31: k1, repeat *, sl5, repeat *, sl5, repeat *, sl5, repeat *, sl5, repeat *, sl5, repeat *, end with k1.
18. Row 32: repeat row 30.
19. Row 33: k1 repeat •, sl6, repeat •, sl6, repeat •, sl6, repeat •, sl6, repeat •, sl5, repeat •, end with k1.
20. Row 34: k 5, sl6, k4, sl6, k4, sl6, k4, sl6 k4, k 5.
21. Row 35: k1, repeat *, sl6, repeat *, sl6, repeat *, sl6, repeat *, sl6, repeat *, end with k1.
22. Row 36: repeat row 30.
23. Row 37: k1, repeat •, sl7, repeat •, sl7, repeat •, sl7, repeat •, sl7, repeat •, end with k1.
24. Row 38: k 5 sl7, k4 sl7, k4 sl7, k4 sl7, k4 sl7, k 5.
25. Row 39: k1, repeat *, sl8, repeat *, sl8, repeat *, sl8, repeat *, sl8, repeat *, end with k1.
26. Row 40: k 5 sl8, k4 sl8, k4 sl8, k4 sl8, k4 sl8, k 5.
27. Row 41: k1, repeat •, sl8, repeat •, sl8, repeat •, sl8, repeat •, sl8, repeat •, end with k1.
28. Row 42: repeat row 30.
29. Row 43: repeat row 35.
30. Row 44: repeat row 30.
31. Row 45: repeat row 37.
32. Row 46: repeat row 30.
33. Row 47: repeat row 35.
34. Row 48: repeat row 30.
35. Row 49: repeat row 37.
36. Row 50: repeat row 30.
37. Row 51: k1, repeat *, sl 9, repeat *, sl 9, repeat *, sl 9, repeat *, sl 9, repeat *, end with k1.
38. Row 52: k 5 sl 9, k4 sl 9, k4 sl 9, k4 sl 9, k4 sl 9, k 5..
39. Row 53: k1, repeat •, sl 9, repeat •, sl 9, repeat •, sl 9, repeat •, sl 9, repeat •, end with k1.
40. Row 54: repeat row 48.
41. Row 55: repeat row 47.
42. Row 56: repeat row 48.
43. Row 57: k1, repeat •, sl10, repeat •, sl10, repeat •, sl10, repeat •, sl10, repeat •, end with k1.
44. Row 58: k 5 sl10, k4 sl10, k4 sl10, k4 sl10, k4 sl10, k 5.

45. Row 59: k1, repeat *, sl10, repeat *, sl10, repeat *, sl10, repeat *, sl10, repeat *, end with k1.
46. Row 60: repeat row 54.
47. Row 61: repeat row 53.
48. Row 62: repeat row 54.
49. Row 63: k1, repeat *, sl11, repeat *, sl11, repeat *, sl11, repeat *, sl11, repeat *, end with k1.
50. Row 64: k 5 sl11, k4 sl11, k4 sl11, k4 sl11, k4 sl11, k 5.
51. Row 65: k1, repeat •, sl11, repeat •, sl11, repeat •, sl11, repeat •, sl11, repeat •, end with k1.
52. Row 66: repeat row 60.
53. Row 67: repeat row 59.
54. Row 68: repeat row 60.
55. Row 69: k1, repeat •, sl12, repeat •, sl12, repeat •, sl12, repeat •, sl12, repeat •, end with k1.
56. Row 70: k 5 sl12, k4 sl12, k4 sl12, k4 sl12, k4 sl12, k 5.
57. Row 71: k1, repeat *, sl12, repeat *, sl12, repeat *, sl12, repeat *, sl12, repeat *, end with k1
58. Row 72: repeat row 66. You're halfway finished! If you prefer a larger purse, add additional rows here.
59. Rows 73 - 144: repeat rows 72 - 1 in that order. When pattern calls for an increase, decrease by knitting two stitches together. Bind off. See Finishing Techniques, p.3.

Two-toned Stripes

Note that this purse is knitted in one piece with two side seams. You begin working on the back side of the purse and end on the front side. Also note that in this purse, two colors of beads and pearl cotton are used to create the pattern.

Supplies:

> ½ hank each of 2 colors of size 11 seed beads
> ½ spool each of 2 colors ofpearl cotton thread
> 8-12 accent beads
> 1 pr. size 0000 knitting needles

Instructions

1. Transfer seed beads onto the pearl cotton thread. Place rubber stoppers on the ends of your knitting needles.
2. Color 1: Cast on 21 stitches.
3. Rows 1 - 4: (color 1) knit across.
4. Rows 5 - 12: (color 1) k1 (*k1 sl1*, rep * 3 x, k3) repeat ( ) , end with k2.
5. Rows 13 - 14: (color 2) k1, *k1 sl1*, rep * across, end with k2.
6. Rows 15 - 22: (color 2) k2 sl1, k3 sl1, k4 sl1, k3 sl1, k4 sl1,k3 sl1, end with k2.
7. Rows 23 - 24: (color 2) repeat rows 13 - 14.
8. Rows 25 - 32: (color 1) k5, (sl1 *k1, sl1*, rep * 3x, k3), rep ( ) 1 x , end with k2.
9. Rows 33 - 45: (color 2) repeat rows 13 - 24.
10. Rows 46 - 54: (color 1) repeat rows 5 - 12.
11. Rows 55 - 61: (color 1) knit across. You're halfway finished!
14. Rows 62 - 122: repeat rows 61 - 1 in that order with the same thread colors listed above.
15. Bind off. See Finishing Techniques, p.3.

Bugle Purse

Supplies:

> 2 hanks size 3 bugle beads
> 300 size 6 seed beads
> ¼ hank size 11 beads
> 1 purse frame 1½ inches deep x 3 inches wide
> 1 pr size 0000 knitting needles

Instructions:

1. To create the fringe pattern strand: Using a flexible eye needle, string a random combination of size 6 and 11 seed beads that is 36 inches in length onto the pearl cotton cord. Measure an additional 3 feet of cord and cut pattern strand from spool of pearl cotton. Set pattern strand aside. Transfer bugle beads onto the pearl cotton thread. Place rubber stoppers on the ends of your knitting needles. Use extra care as you slide beads down the cord (bugle beads have sharp edges).

2. Using the overhand method, cast on 4 stitches, sl1, repeat across 5 times, end with co4. (You should have 24 stitches and 5 beads.)

3. Rows 1 - 24: k4, sl1 across, ending with k4.

4. Row 25: *k1 inc1, k3 sl1*, repeat * 5 times, ending with k1 inc1, k3.

5. Rows 26 - 36: *k5 sl1*, repeat * 5 times, ending with k5.

6. Row 37: *k1 inc1, k4 sl1*, repeat * 5 times, ending with k1 inc1, k4.

7. Rows 38 - 46: *k6 sl1*, repeat * 5 times, ending with k6.

8. Row 47 : *k1 inc1, k5 sl1*, repeat 5 times, ending with k1 inc1, k5.

9. Rows 48 - 56: *k7 sl1*, repeat 5 times, ending with k7.

10. Row 57: *k1 inc1, k6 sl1*, repeat 5 times, ending with k1 inc1, k6.

11. Rows 58 - 66: *k8 sl1*, repeat * 5 times, ending with k8. Measure purse length; if additional length is needed, add extra rows here.

12. Row 67: k8, slide a 4 inch section of beads (so that fringe will measure 2 inches); repeat across, ending with k8.

13. Row 68: *k8 sl1*, repeat * 5 times, ending with k8. Cut strand leaving an 8 inch tail.

14. Row 69: using pattern strand of size 6 and 11 seed beads: k8 slide a 3 inch section of beads; repeat across, ending with k8.

15. Row 70: using the pattern strand,* k 8, slide a combination of 6 & 11 beads similar in size to 1 bugle*; repeat

47

* 5 times, end with k8. Cut strand, remove unused beads and leave an 8 inch tail.
16. Rows 71 - 139: using main strand with bugle beads repeat rows 68 - 1 in that order.
17. Cast off all stitches, leaving one stitch in each sequence on the needle and tails of thread for each section. Tie off last stitch with tail and weave ends into knitting. Tie off all knots from fringe and dab with glue. See Finishing Techniques, p.3.

Matchbox

Note that this purse is knitted in one piece with two gussets. Use extra care as you slide beads down the cord (bugle beads have sharp edges).

Supplies:
     ½ hank size 3 "bugle beads"(½ inch)
     ½ spool pearl cotton
     8-12 decorative beads
     1 pr. size 0000 knitting needles

Instructions:
1. Transfer bugle beads onto cotton thread (you will use 1/2 hank of bugle beads). Place rubber stoppers on the ends of knitting needles.
2. Row 1: *Cast on 3 stitches. Slide 1 bead *. Repeat * 2 times, end with cast on 3 stitches. (I use the overhand method of casting on for ease).
3. Rows 2 - 83: * knit 3 sl1*, repeat * 2 times, end with knit 3. It is important to keep stitches fairly even on the first two rows.
4. Row 84: bind off as follows: *k2 co1,k1 co1* (1 st will remain on needles), repeat * 2 times, k2 co1, k1 co1. Break thread leaving an 8 inch tail. Tie off last stitch with tail. You will have 3 stitches remaining on your knitting needles. Thread flexible eye needle with 8 inch tail. Weave thread through bugle beads and through the loops. Tie off at side.

Gussets: (make two of these)
1. Row 1: cast on 2 st, sl1 bead, co 2.
2. Rows 2 - 40: k2, sl1, k2.
3. Bind off the same as with purse body.

Purse Assembly: with wrong sides together, sew purse gussets to sides using pearl cotton thread. (Leave open at bottom where bugle bead gusset meets purse.) Tie off in square knots and dab with glue. Weave ends into seams, if possible. See Finishing Techniques, p.3.

     49

Seed Stitch

Note that it is especially important to remember to move your thread from the back to the front of your work before each purl stitch, and from front to back before knit stitches.

Supplies:

1 hank of size 11 seed beads
1 spool of pearl cotton thread

1 pr. size 0000 knitting needles
8-20 decorative beads

Instructions

1. Cast on 20 stitches.
2. Rows 1 - 3: knit across, end with p1.
3. Rows 4, 6, 8 & 10: k1, p1 across.
4. Rows 5, 7, 9 & 11: knit across.
5. Row 12: * k1 p1, k1 p1, sl1*, repeat * across, end with k1, p1, k1, p1. Note: beads slide to back side of work. Take thread to back preparing for k st, then slide the bead.
6. Row 13: k4 sl1, repeat across, end with k4.
7. Row 14: * k1 p1, k1, p1 sl2*, repeat * across, end with k1, p1, k1, p1.
8. Row 15: k4 sl2, repeat across, end with k4.
9. Row 16: * k1 p1, k1 p1, sl3*, repeat * across, end with k1, p1, k1, p1.
10. Row 17: k4 sl3, repeat across, end with k4.
11. Row 18: * k1 p1, k1 p1, sl4*, repeat * across, end with k1, p1, k1, p1.
12. Row 19: k4 sl4, repeat across, end with k4.
13. Row 20: * k1 p1, k1 p1, sl5*, repeat * across, end with k1, p1, k1, p1.
14. Row 21: k4 sl5, repeat across, end with k4.
15. Row 22: repeat row 20.
16. Row 23: repeat row 21.
17. Rows 24, 26, 28 &30: * k1 p1, k1 p1, sl6*, repeat * across, end with k1, p1, k1, p1.
18. Rows 25, 27, 29 & 31: k4 sl6, repeat across, end with k4.
19. Rows 32, 34, 36, 38 & 40: * k1 p1, k1 p1, sl7*, repeat * across, end with k1, p1, k1, p1.
20. Rows 33, 35, 37, 39 & 41: k4 sl7, repeat across, end with k4. (You are halfway finished!)
22. Rows 42 - 82 repeat rows 40 - 1 in that order.
23. Bind off. See Finishing Techniques, p.3.

Porcupine

Be careful when sliding bugle beads down thread as they have a tendency to cut the thread.

Supplies:

½ hank size 3 "bugle beads"
½ ball pearl cotton thread
1 pr size 0000 knitting needles

Instructions

Purse Back:

1. Pull one end of one strand of bugle beads out from the hank's knot. Tie an overhand knot with the strand from the hank of bugle beads onto the pearl cotton thread. Slide beads onto pearl cotton thread from the strand of the hank of beads. You will use most of the hank of beads. Place rubber stoppers on the ends of knitting needles.
2. Row 1: *Cast on 4 stitches. Slide 1 bead*. Repeat * 1 time, end with cast on 4 stitches. (I used the overhand method of casting on for ease). Refer to any knitting book for instructions on this method.
3. Rows 2 - 42: * knit 4 sl1*, repeat * once, end with knit 4. It is important to keep stitches fairly even on the first two rows.
4. Row 84: bind off as follows: *k2 co1,k1 co1,k1 co1* (1 st will remain on needles), repeat * once, k2 co1, k1 co1, k1 co1. Break thread leaving an 8 inch tail. Tie off last stitch with tail. You will have 3 st remaining on your knitting needles. Thread flexible eye needle with 8 inch tail. Weave thread through bugle beads and through the loops. Tie off at side.

Purse Front:
1. Cast on 18 stitches.
2. Rows 1 - 7:   knit across.
3. Row 8 and all even rows through 28:   k2 sl2, end with k2.
4. Rows 9 and all odd rows through 27:   knit across.
5. Row 29:   k1, k2 together, k across (17 stitches).
6. Row 30:   k1, k2 tog, * sl2 k2*, rep * across, end with k2 (16 stitches).
7. Rows 31 and all odd rows through 39:   knit across
8. Rows 32 and all even rows through 40:   k2 sl2, repeat across end with k2.
9. Rows 41 - 42:   knit across.
10. Bind off.

Purse Assembly: With wrong sides together, whip stitch side seams and bottom. Tie off in square knots and dab with glue. Weave ends into seams, if possible. See Finishing Techniques. I chose to add a beaded drop from the bottom of this purse by securing thread to the bottom side of the purse, then threading 1 seed bead, a bugle bead, a seed bead, a star charm bead, a seed bead, the teardrop bead, a seed bead; then returning through the teardrop bead, seed bead, star bead, seed bead; then adding a bugle bead, seed bead and securing this to the other bottom side of the purse. See Finishing Techniques, p.3.

Web Stitch

This is my favorite pattern to knit! I enjoy the loose web-like strands stretching in between the sections of beads. I found that it is difficult to change colors of thread in this pattern without making knots to secure the new color. It is important to maintain the correct tension throughout the piece, thus the knots.

Supplies:

3 ¼ hanks each size 11 seed beads   one 2-inch wide purse frame
3 ½ spools of pearl cotton thread   8-12 decorative beads
1 pr size 0000 knitting needles

Instructions

1. Transfer 3 colors of beads onto 3 colors of cotton thread. You will use approximately 3 16-inch strands of beads for each color of thread. Place rubber stoppers on the ends of knitting needles.
2. Cast on 28 stitches using color #1.
3. Rows 1 - 7: knit across.
4. Rows 8, 10 & 12 & 14: *k1, slp2 purlwise, k1, slp 2, sl4*, rep * 3x, k1 slp 2, k1.
5. Row 9 and all odd rows: knit across.
6. Rows 16,18 & 20 & 22: (using color #2) *k1, slp 2, sl4, k1, slp2*, repeat * 3x, end with k1,sl2, k1.
7. Rows 24, 26, 28 & 30: (using color #1) repeat rows 8 - 14.
8. Rows 32, 34 , 36 & 38: (using color #3) repeat rows 16 - 22.
9. Rows 40, 42,44 & 46: (using color #2) repeat rows 8 - 14.
10. Rows 48, 50, 52 & 58: (using color #1) repeat rows 16 - 22.
11. Rows 60, 62, 64 & 68: (using color #3) repeat rows 8 - 14.
12. Row 70: (using color #3) *k1, sl35, k1*, repeat across, end with k2.
13. Row 72: (using color #2) *k2, sl30*, repeat across, end with k1.
14. Row 74: (using color #3) *k1, sl25, k1*, repeat across, end with k2.
15. Rows 75 - 150: repeat rows 74 - 1 in descending order.
16. Bind off. Tie all thread ends in square knots. Dab with glue. Leave tails at least 3 inches (this will help with assembly). With wrong sides together, sew purse side that has the knots first using color #1. Be careful not to catch the loops as you sew.On other side, with wrong sides together, sew purse side. Tie off in square knots and dab with glue. Weave ends into seams, if possible. See Finishing Techniques, p.3.

Three Purse Flaps

These should be knitted first, before the body of the purse. All patterns have variations for 18, 20 and 24 stitch purses featured in this book. Note: all increases are made in the proceeding knit stitch by first knitting, then before you take the stitch off the needle, placing the right hand needle into the back of the same stitch, knitting it to create a second stitch.

Supplies:

> size 11 seed beads
> size 8 pearl cotton to match project
> 1 pr size 0000 knitting needles

Dotted Flap Instructions

1. Cast on 4 stitches.
2. Rows 1 - 2: k across.
3. Row 3:   k2, sl1, k2 (4 stitches)
4. Row 4:   k across.
5. Row 5:   *k1 inc1, sl1*, rep * 2x, k1 inc1. (8 stitches)
6. Row 6:   k across.
7. Row 7:   *k1 inc1, sl1* rep * 1x, k2 sl1, k2 sl1, k1 inc1, sl1 k1 inc1. (12 stitches)
8. Row 8:   k across.
9. Row 9:   *k1 inc1, sl1* rep 1x, *k2, sl1* repeat * 3 x, k1 inc1 sl1 ,k1 inc. (16 stitches)
10. Row 10: k across.
11. Row 11: k1 inc1, sl1, *k2, sl1* repeat * 5x, k1, inc1 sl1, k1 inc1.(18 stitches)
12. Row 12: k across.
13. Row 13: k2 sl1, repeat across.
14. Row 14: k across.
15. Row 15: k2 sl1, repeat across.
16. Row 16: k across.
17. Row 17: **For 18 stitch purses**: k2, sl1 across; proceed to purse instructions featured in this book.

For 20 stitch purses: k1 inc. 1, *sl1 k2*, repeat *5x, k1 inc 1, sl1, k1 inc1, then proceed to step 18 below. Then proceed to purse instructions.

18. Rows18 &19: k across.

    For 24 stitch purses:

19. Row 20: k1, inc 1, *sl1 k2*, repeat * 8x, k1, inc 1, sl1 k1 inc1.(24 stitches)

20. Row 21 - 26: knit across. Proceed to purse instructions featured in this book.

Striped Flap Instructions:

1. Cast on 4 stitches.
2. Rows 1 - 2: k across.
3. Row 3: k1 inc1, k1 sl1, k1 inc1, k1. (6 stitches)
4. Row 4: k across.
5. Row 5: k1 inc1, sl1, k2 sl2, k2 sl1,k1 sl1, inc1, k1. (8 stitches)
6. Row 6: k across.
7. Row 7: k1 inc1 sl1, k1 inc1, sl1, k2 sl1, k2 sl1, k1 inc1, sl1, k1 inc1. (12 stitches)
8. Row 8: k across.
9. Row 9: *k1 inc1, sl1*, rep * 1x, *k2 sl1*, rep * 4 x, k1 inc1 sl1, k1 inc1. (16 stitches)
10. Row 10: k across.
11. Row 11: k1 inc1, k1 sl1, *k2 sl1*, repeat * 5x, k2, k1 inc1. (18 stitches).
12. Row 12: k across.
13. Row 13: k1sl1, *k2 sl1* rep * across, end with k1. (18 stitches)
14. Rows 14, 16 &18: k across.
15. Rows 15, 17 & 19: rep row 13.
16. Row 20: **For 18 stitch purses:** k across. Proceed to purse instructions (omit cast on).

    For 20 stitch purses: k1 inc1, k across, repeat on Row 21, then continue to purse instructions.

    For 24 stitch purses: k1 inc1, k1 inc1, knit across, repeat on Row 21, then continue to small purse instructions featured in this book.

Diamond Flap Instructions:

1. Cast on 2 stitches.
2. Row 1 - 3: k1 inc1, k across, end with inc1 k1.
3. Row 4: k4 sl1, k4.
4. Row 5: k1 inc 1, k3 sl1, k3 inc1, end with k1.
5. Row 6: k1 inc1, sl1 k4, sl2 k4, sl1 inc1, end with k1.
6. Row 7: k1 inc1, k1 sl1, k4 sl2, k4 sl1, k1 inc1, end with k1
7. Row 8: k1 inc1, k2 sl2, k4 sl3, k4 sl2, k2 inc1, end with k1.
8. Row 9: k1 inc1, k3 sl2, k4 sl3, k4 sl2, k3 inc1, end with k1.
9. Row 10: k5 sl2, k4 sl3, k4 sl2, end with k5.(18 stitches)
10. Rows 11 - 12: k5 sl1, k4 sl2, k4 sl1, end with k5.
11. Rows 13 - 14: k9 sl1, k9. **(for 20 stitch purses**, inc 1 stitch after first stitch and before last stitch in row 13 only).
12. Rows 15 - 22: k across. **(For 24 stitch purses**, inc 1 stitch after first stitch in each row during first 4 rows). Proceed to purse instructions featured in this book. (Do not bind off or remove knitting from needles). See Finishing Techniques, p.3.

Patchwork Quilt

Supplies:

        4 colors size 11 seed beads ¼ hank each
        4 colors size 8 pearl cotton
        1 color size 3 bugle beads ¼ hank
        1 ½" x 2 ½" purse frame
        small 6"x 6" square of flannel
        1 pr. size 0000 knitting needles

Instructions:

Slide beads onto pearl cotton thread from the strand of the hank of beads. Do this for each color of thread that you will be using and transfer two 16-inch strands to start with (approximately three 16-inch strands of beads for each color of thread). Keep your spools of cotton thread separately in small baggies and only slide the beads down about 1 foot at a time while knitting to prevent tangling. Place rubber stoppers on the ends of knitting needles.

Purse Top: (Make one of these, or two if you plan to knit both sides of the purse. Allow 1/2 ball of cotton for these and use one color of size 11 seed beads that contrast. This can be the same thread color that you will use later to join all quilt squares.)

1. Cast on 28 stitches.
2. Rows 1 - 10:   knit across.
3. Row 11 & 12: k 6, sl1, *k4, sl1*, repeat * across, end with k 6.
4. Row 13 & 14: k 5, sl1, *k2, sl1*,repeat * across, end with k5.
5. Rows 15 &16: k4, sl1, *k4 sl1*, repeat * across, end with knit 4.
6. Row 17 &18: repeat rows 15 & 16.
7. Row 19 & 20: repeat rows 11 &12.
8. Row 21 & 22: repeat rows 11 & 12.
9. Row 23 & 24: repeat rows 13& 14.
10. Row 25 & 26: repeat rows 15 & 16.

11. Row 27 & 28:   repeat rows 15 & 16.
12. Rows 29 - 30: repeat rows 13 - 14.
13. Rows 31 - 32: repeat rows 11- 12.
15. Rows 33 - 35: knit across.
16. Row 36: bind off loosely.

Purse Body:

The purse body is constructed out of squares of beaded knit patterns using various colors of thread and beads to create a patchwork quilt effect. Pick and choose the colors and pattern squares that you wish to use. Make a total of 32 squares for the front and back sides of the purse (or 16, if you prefer the squares to be on the front only).

Pattern Square #1: Dots (using size 11 seed beads on cotton cord).
1.   Cast on 7 stitches.
2.   Row 1: knit across
3.   Row 2: k3, sl1, k1,sl1,k3.
4.   Row 3: knit across.
5.   Row 4: k4,sl1,k1, sl1,k2.
6.   Row 5: knit across.
7.   Row 6: repeat row 2..
8.   Row 7: knit across.
9.   Row 8: repeat row 3.
10. Row 9: knit across.
11. Row 10: repeat row 2.
12. Row 11: knit across.
13. Row 12: repeat row 3.
14. Row 13: knit across.
15. Row 14: repeat row 2.
16. Row 15: knit across.
17. Row 16: bind off.

Pattern Square #2: Heart (using size 11 seed beads on cotton cord). Cast on 10 stitches.
1.   Rows 1 - 2: knit across.
2.   Rows 3 - 4: k4, sl1, k3 sl1, k4.
3.   Rows 5 - 8: k2, sl1 across, end with k2.
4.   Rows 9 - 10: k3, sl1, k4, sl1, k3.
5.   Rows 11 & 12: k4, sl1, k2, sl1, k4.
6.   Row 13 & 14: k5, sl1, k5.
7.   Row 17: knit across.
8.   Row 18: bind off.

Pattern Square #3: Loops (using size 11 seed beads on cotton cord). Cast on 8 stitches.
1.   Row 1 & 2: knit across.
2.   Rows 3, 5, 7, 9 & 11: k3, sl10, k1,sl10, k1, sl10, k3.
3.   Rows 4, 6, 8, 10, 12 & 14 - 15: knit across.
4.   Row 16: bind off.

Pattern Square #4: Porcupine (using size 3 bugle beads on cotton cord). Cast on 8 stitches.
1.   Rows 1 - 2: knit across.
2.   Rows 3, 5, 7, 9 & 11, 13: k2, sl2, *k1 sl2*, repeat * across ending with k2.
3.   Rows 4, 6, 8, 10, 12 & 14 - 15: knit across.
4.   Row 16: bind off.

Pattern Square #5: Bugles (using size 3 bugle beads on cotton cord).
1.   Cast on 3 stitches, sl1 bugle, cast on 3 stitches.
2.   Rows 1 - 15: k3, sl1, k3.
3.   Row 16: bind off 3, cut thread, with new thread bind off 3. Secure ends.

Pattern Square #6: Criss-cross (using size 11 seed beads on cotton cord).
1.   Rows 1 - 2:   knit across.
2.   Rows 3 - 4:   k2, sl1, k4, sl1, k2.
3.   Rows 5 - 6:   k3, sl1, k2, sl1, k3.
4.   Rows 7 - 10:   k4, sl2, k2, k4.
5.   Rows 11 - 12: repeat rows 5 & 6
6.   Rows 13 - 14: repeat rows 3 & 4.
7.   Rows 15 - 16: knit across.

Purse Assembly:
1.   Arrange squares into 2 sets of rows of 4, columns of 4 (1 set for each side), so that colors and patterns vary from row to column. With right sides together, join squares by straight stitching or back stitching, using the same color of thread used for the purse top. You will now have two sections of 4" x 4" squares. Attach these two sections (creating the purse bottom) by 4 rows of sc. Dab all knots with glue, keep all ends on the inside of the purse, and clip all threads. Join purse tops to squares using 3 rows of sc with same color of thread. With right sides together, whip stitch purse sides together, leaving the top sides open where it will attach to the frame. It is important to catch only one stitch on the sides of the purse, so that the pattern of the squares located on the edges are not lost.
2.   To attach purse top to frame: See Finishing Techniques, p.3.

The Flower

Note that this purse features 2 colors of cotton thread and two colors of seed beads. It is knit in two sections that are later joined together. An optional component uses a third color in small amounts of both thread and seed beads (see instructions).

Supplies:

> 1 hank main color seed beads
> ½ hank lighter color seed beads
> ½ spool main color size 8 pearl cotton
> 1/3 spool lighter color size 8 pearl cotton
> 5 – 7 glass leaf beads, 12 various color decorative beads for strap and bottom fringe
> (Optional: 4 yards green or yellow thread, 2 strands of similar colored seed beads).

Instructions:

Transfer seed beads onto cotton thread as follows: darker main color thread will use 3/4 of a hank of the darker color seed beads; lighter color thread will use 1/2 hank of lighter color seed beads.

Purse Body (using darker main color of thread/beads):

1. Cast on 9 stitches.
2. Row 1: k across.
3. Rows 2 - 3: k1, sl1, repeat across (7 times), ending with k1.
4. Row 4: k1, in this stitch inc1, sl1, repeat across (7 times), ending with k1, inc1.
   (Remember, you slide the bead after you increase as you begin to knit the next stitch. There will be 2 stitches between each bead).
5. Row 5: k2, sl1, repeat across, end with k 2.
6. Row 6: k2, sl1,* k2 in 2nd stitch inc1, sl1 *, repeat * across, end with k2. There will be 3 stitches between each bead.
7. Rows 7 - 10: k2, sl1, * k3, sl1*, repeat * across, end with k2.
8. Rows 11 - 14: k2, sl2, * k3, sl2*, repeat * across, end with k2.

9. Rows 15 - 16: k2, sl3, *k3, sl3*, repeat * across, end with k2.
10. Rows 17 - 18: k2, sl4, *k3, sl4*, repeat * across, end with k2.
11. Rows 19 - 22: k2, sl5, *k3, sl5*, repeat * across, end with k2.
12. Rows 23 - 28: k2, sl6, *k3, sl6*, repeat * across, end with k2.
13. Rows 29 - 34: k2, sl7, *k3, sl7*, repeat * across, end with k2.
14. Rows 35 - 40: k2, sl8, *k3, sl8*, repeat * across, end with k2.
15. Rows 41 - 46: k2, sl7, *k3, sl7*, repeat * across, end with k2.
16. Rows 47 - 52: k2, sl6, *k3, sl6*, repeat * across, end with k2.
17. Row 53: k2, sl5, *k3, sl5*, repeat * across, end with k2.
18. Row 54: k2, * sl5, k2 in second stitch inc1, k1 *, repeat * across, end with sl5, k2.
19. Row 55: k2, sl5, k4, sl5, k2 (keep all other stitches on needle or stitch holder). Place rubber stoppers on needle to prevent stitches from sliding off. Turn work. You will begin making each petal. There will be a total of 4 petals.
20. Row 56: with new needle, k2, sl5, k4, sl5, end with k2.
21. Rows 57 - 62: k2, sl4, k4, sl4, end with k2.
22. Rows 63 - 72: k2, sl3, k4, sl3, end with k2.
23. Rows 73 - 76: k2, sl2, k4, sl2, end with k2.
24. Rows 77 – 80: k2, sl1, k4, sl1, end with k2.
25. Row 81: k2tog 4 times. You should have four stitches left on your needle.
26. Row 82: K2tog twice. Bind off. Your first petal is complete.
27. Return to stitches held on needle or stitch holder. Reattach thread with beads and repeat rows 55 – 82 and step 27 for each of the three remaining petals for the main body.

Inside petals using lighter main color of thread and beads:
1. Cast on 37 stitches loosely.
2. Rows 1 - 8: k2, * sl5, k3*, repeat * across ending with k2. (There will be 12 bead segments.)
3. Row 9 - 10: k2, sl5, k3, sl5, k1, inc1. (Keep all other stitches on needle or stitch holder.)

Place rubber stoppers on needle to prevent stitches from sliding off. Turn work. You will begin making each inside petal now. There are a total of 6 inside petals.

4. Rows 11 - 16: k2, sl4, k3, sl4, k2.
5. Rows 17 – 28: k2, sl3, k3, sl3, k2.
6. Rows 29 – 34: k2, sl2, k3, sl2, k2.
7. Rows 35 – 36: k2, sl1, k3, sl1, k2.
8. Row 37: k2 tog across, ending with k1. (You will have 4 stitches left on your needle.)
9. Row 38: k2 tog twice. Bind off. Leave a 6-inch tail of thread. Your first petal is complete! Reattach lighter color of pearl cotton thread and repeat steps 2 through 9 (rows 9 – 38) for each of the 5 remaining petals.

Pattern variation to create a lighter stripe down the inside petals (read all instructions first):

1. Place three strands of yellow or green seed beads onto yellow or green pearl cotton. Cut green thread into sections of six 2-foot sections containing 40 seed beads each. Each strand will be used on each petal to create a green stripe between the sections of lighter main color beads on the inside petals.
2. With lighter main color of thread, cast on 37 stitches loosely.
3. Rows 1 - 8: k2, *sl5, k1. Change to green/yellow thread and seed beads, sl1, k1*. Change back to lighter main color k1, repeat * across, always beginning with lighter main color and incorporating each of the 6 new strands of green cord each time, ending with k2.
4. Row 9 - 10: k2, sl5, k1. Change to green/yellow thread and seed beads, k1. Change back to lighter main color: k1, sl5, ending with k2. (Keep all other stitches on needle or stitch holder.) Place rubber stoppers on needle to prevent stitches from sliding off. Turn work. (You will begin making each petal now. There are a total of 6 inside petals.)
5. Rows 11 – 16: k2, sl5, k1. Change to green/yellow thread and seed beads, sl1, k1. Change back to lighter main color: k1, sl5, k2.
6. Rows 17 – 28: k2, sl4, k1. Change to green/yellow thread and seed beads, sl1, k1. Change back to lighter main color: k1, sl4, k2.

63

7. Rows 29 – 34: k2, sl2, k1. Change to green/yellow thread and seed beads, sl1, k1. Change back to lighter main color: k1, sl2, k2.
8. Rows 35 – 36: k2, sl1, k1. Change to green/yellow thread and seed beads, sl1, k1. Change back to lighter main color: k1, sl1, k2.
9. Row 37: k2 tog across. (You will have 4 stitches remaining on your needle.)
10. Row 38: K2 tog. Bind off. Leave a 6-inch tail of thread. Your first petal is complete!
   Repeat steps 2 through 10 (rows 9 – 38) for each of the 5 remaining petals.

Purse assembly:

Weave ends of threads from the base of each petal into knitting. To embellish tips of petals, weave thread tails to center and attach beads. Lay out the main purse body with "wrong" side facing you. (Wrong side can be the one with mistakes.) Place the inside petals on top of the main purse body with "right" side facing you. Petals will overlap. It is best to tack them at a point where the inside petals are ¼" longer than outside petals. Tack as follows: at edges, in the middle of the second inside petals, and between the three inside petals (these should line up with sections of knitting on the outside petals). Once assembled, this will allow inside petals to hang at approximately the same length as the outside petals. Using darker color of thread (the same color as the main purse body), attach main purse body to lighter purse petals on knit stitch areas by tacking them together. Knots should be on the side facing you (inside of purse). Next, turn purse inside out and whip stitch the main seam of the purse to the beginning of petals. Trim off excess thread, dab all knots with glue. Stuff a charm or cotton ball into purse body to fill it. Attach beads or charms to the purse bottom as desired, using size B Nymo thread and a size 12 beading needle. Assemble strap so that purse seam is in the back middle of purse. See Finishing Techniques, p.3 for strap assembly.

Project Notes:

Project Notes:

Project Notes:

❧ Project Notes: ❧

Abbreviations:

k = knit

sl = slide (a bead)

inc = increase

dec = decrease by knitting two stitches together

db = decorative bead

p = purl

sc = single crochet

dc = double crochet

rep = repeat sequence

co = cast on a stitch

cof = cast off

tog = together

slp = slip stitch purlwise

bo = bind off

st = stitch

Guide to Photographic Images

Front Cover: "The Flower"

Inside Pages:

7. Left: "Dottie Loop", Center: "Simply Lovely", Right: "Lacey"

8. Left: "The Lantern", Center: "The Dress", Right: "Seed Stitch"

9. Left: "Dotted Coin Purse", Right: "The Vase"

10. Left: "Zig Zag", Center: Diamonds", Right: Two-tone Zig"

11. Left: "Pinstripes", Center: "Pinstripes" on a frame, Right: "Mini Pinstripes"

12. Left: "Heart", Center: "Two-toned Stripe", Right: "Web Stitch"

13. Left: "Matchbox", Right: "Bugle Purse", Below: "Porcupine"

14. Left: "The Flower", Center: "The Quilt", Right: "Sachet"

Back Cover: "The Flower", "The Quilt", "Sachet"